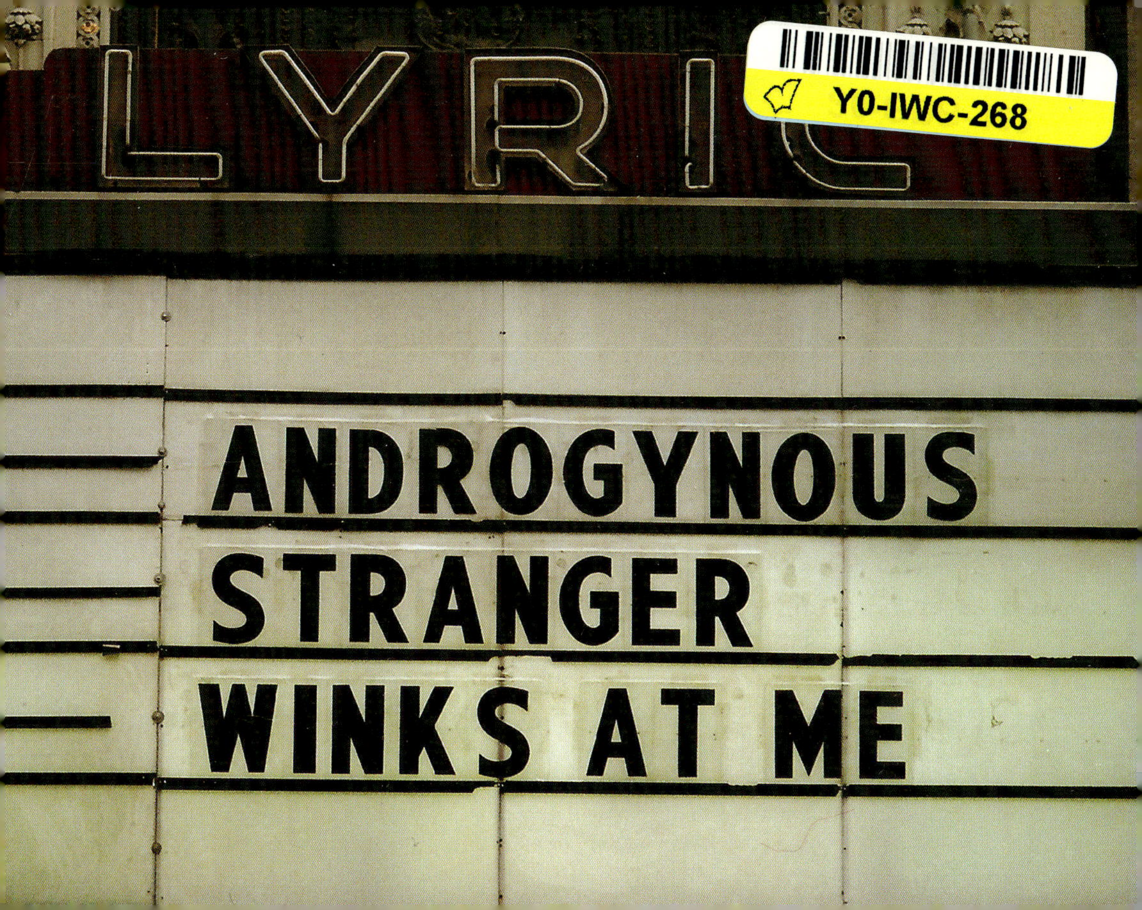
LYRIC
ANDROGYNOUS
STRANGER
WINKS AT ME

Androgynous – haiku by Karen Sohne

Haiku on 42nd Street, Clerisy Press

DOLL HOSPITAL
THE MAN BRINGS OUT
A TRAY
OF NEW BLUE EYES

Doll Hospital – haiku by Patricia Neubauer

Haiku on 42nd Street, Clerisy Press

Empire
ON THE TWELFTH FLOOR
A LIFE'S WORK HOLDS OPEN
THE BOOK REVIEWER'S DOOR

On the twelfth floor – haiku by Martin Burke

Haiku on 42nd Street, Clerisy Press

ONE ADMISSION PRICE
ORION
HAS HE PUT
ON WEIGHT?

Orion – haiku by Carl Patrick

Haiku on 42nd Street, Clerisy Press

HARRIS
CITY STREET
MY SUITCASE BUMPS
HIS CARDBOARD BOX

City Street – haiku by Minna Lerman

Haiku on 42nd Street, Clerisy Press

CAR PILED WITH LUGGAGE
STRAYING INTO THE FUNERAL
PROCESSION

Car piled with Luggage – haiku by Yvonne Hardenbrook

Haiku on 42nd Street, Clerisy Press

ROXY
SLOWLY RECOGNIZING
A LARGE DOG
IN THE CAR AHEAD

Slowly recognizing – haiku by Penny Harter

Haiku on 42nd Street, Clerisy Press

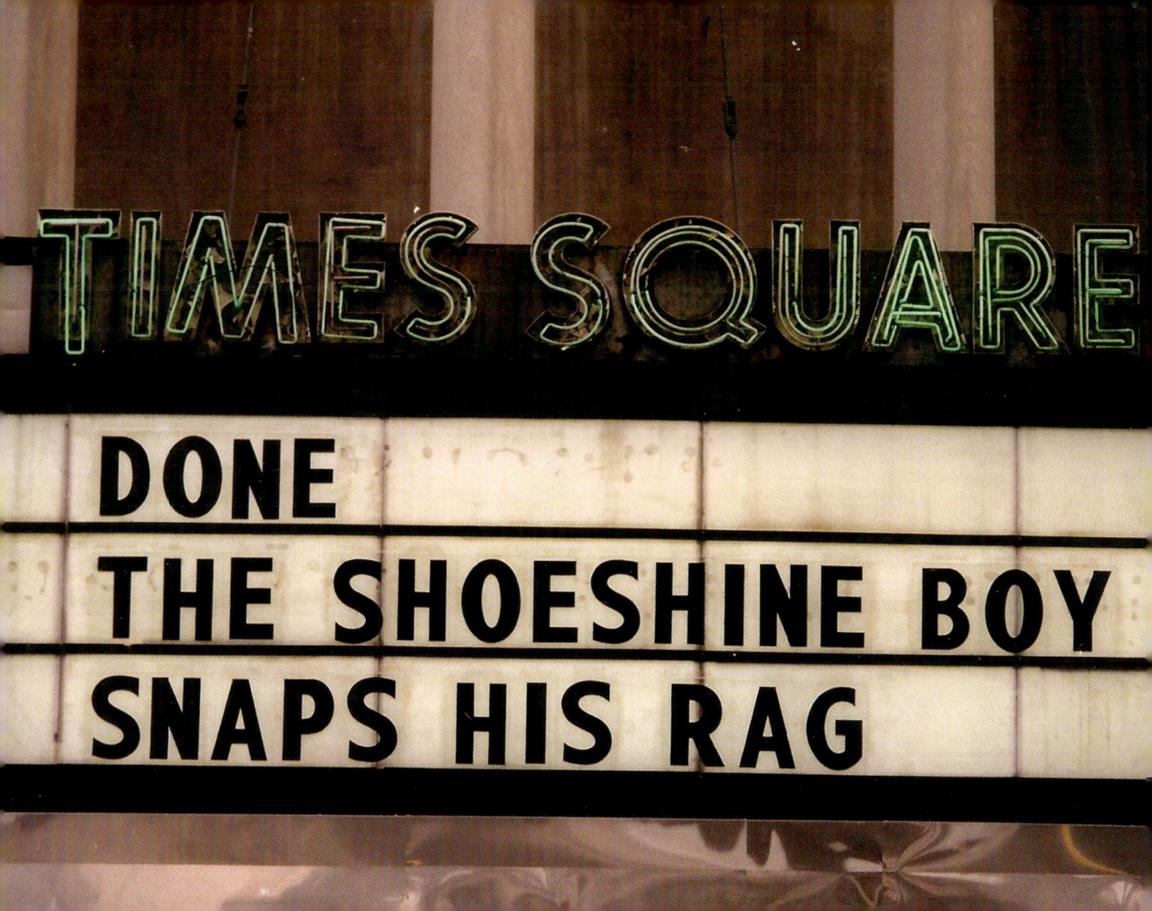
TIMES SQUARE
DONE
THE SHOESHINE BOY
SNAPS HIS RAG

Done – haiku by Alan Pizzarelli

Haiku on 42nd Street, Clerisy Press

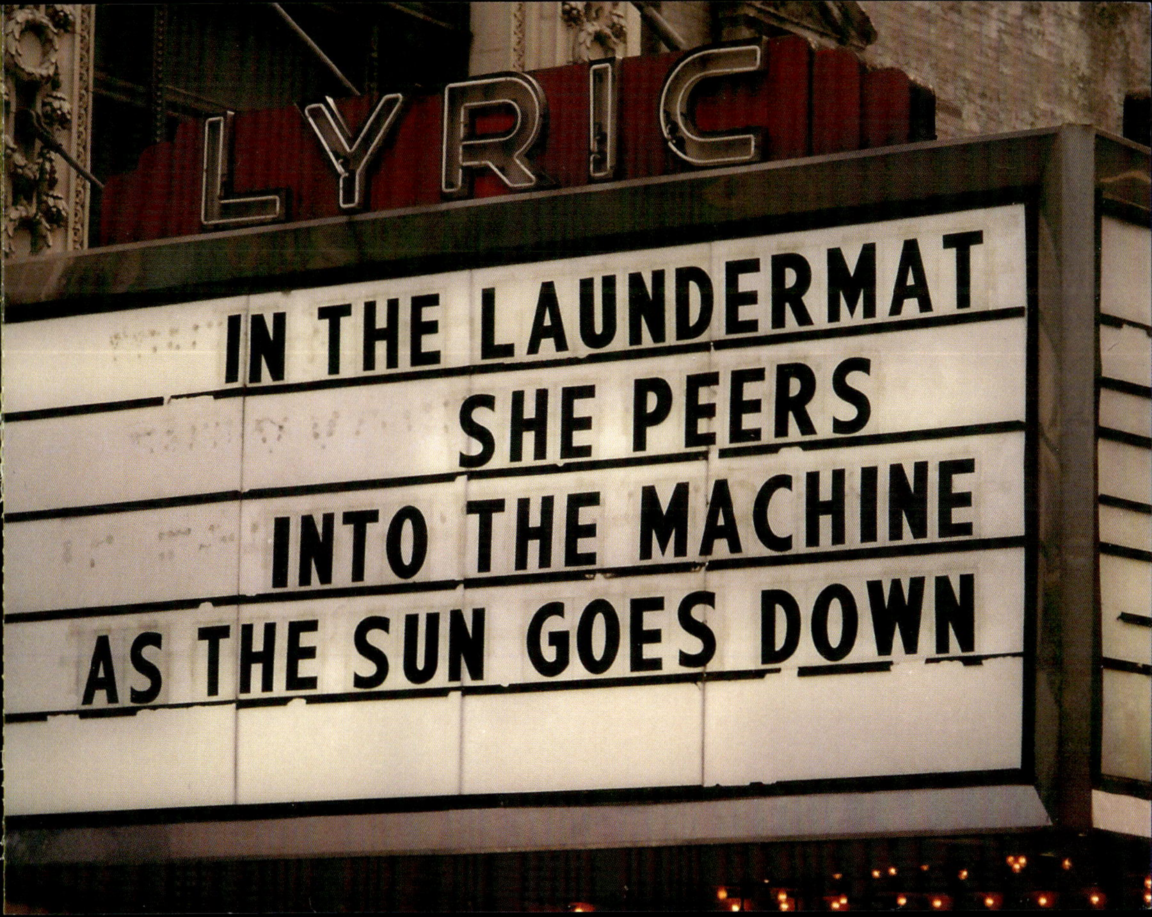
LYRIC
IN THE LAUNDERMAT
SHE PEERS
INTO THE MACHINE
AS THE SUN GOES DOWN

Haiku on 42nd Street, Clerisy Press

CINE 42
HOT DAY
UNDER TIGHT
WHITE SLACKS
JUST HER

Hot day – haiku by L.A. Davidson

Haiku on 42nd Street, Clerisy Press

BETWEEN THE MOON
AND THE BILLBOARD
A JET LINER RISING

Haiku on 42nd Street, Clerisy Press

CINE
WITH HIS CLIPPERS
THE FLORIST PRUNES
HIS CIGAR

With his clippers – haiku by Even Mahl

Haiku on 42nd Street, Clerisy Press

MY REFLECTION
SPLATTERED
BY THE CITY BUS
ONTO MY PANTS

My reflection – haiku by Mykel Board

Haiku on 42nd Street, Clerisy Press

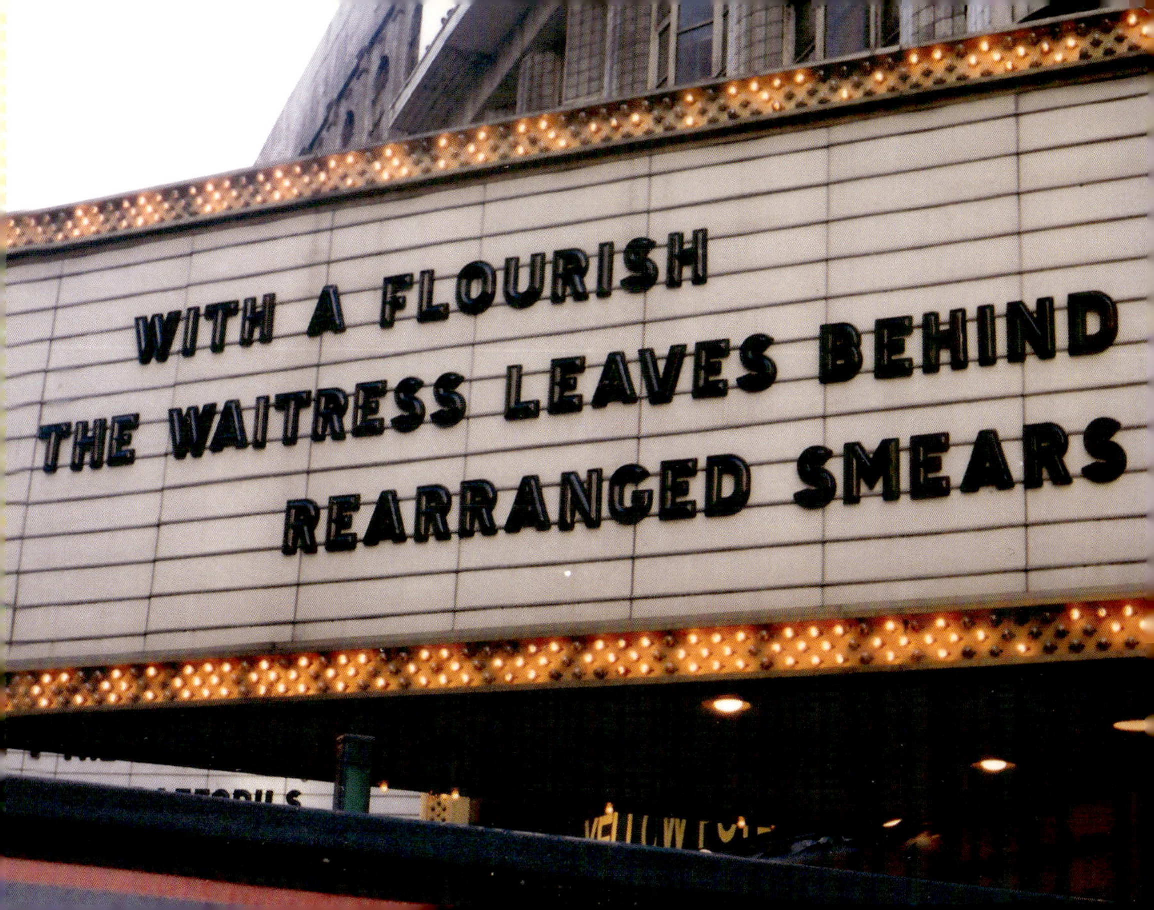
WITH A FLOURISH
THE WAITRESS LEAVES BEHIND
REARRANGED SMEARS

With a flourish – haiku by Dee Evetts

Haiku on 42nd Street, Clerisy Press

Liberty
THE DRIVER
PALMS HIS CIGARETTE
OPENS
THE HEARSE DOOR

The driver – haiku by Anita Virgil

Haiku on 42nd Street, Clerisy Press

LYRIC
IN GREENWICH VILLAGE
TOURISTS ASKING
HOW TO GET
TO GREENWICH VILLAGE

In Greenwich Village – haiku by Bernard Lionel Einbond

Haiku on 42nd Street, Clerisy Press

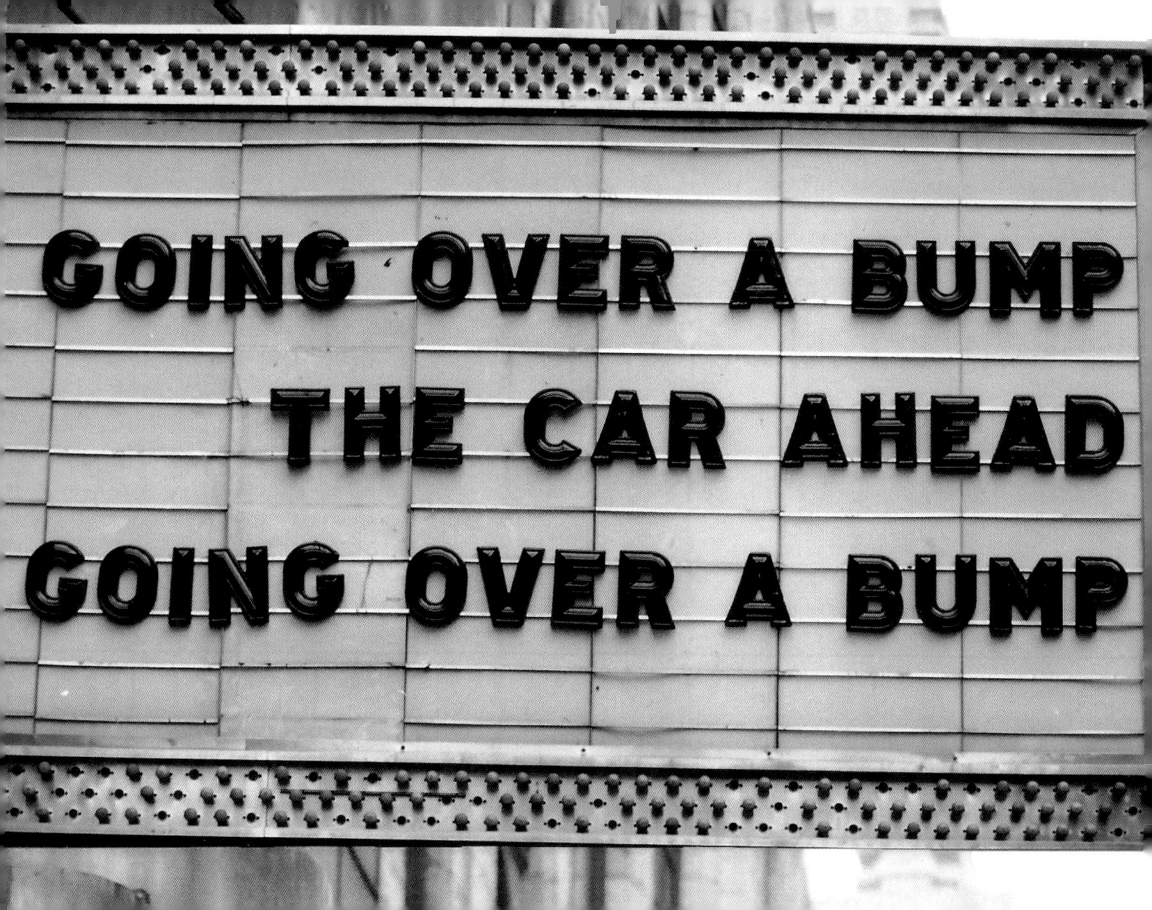
GOING OVER A BUMP
THE CAR AHEAD
GOING OVER A BUMP

Going over a bump – haiku by William J. Higginson

Haiku on 42nd Street, Clerisy Press

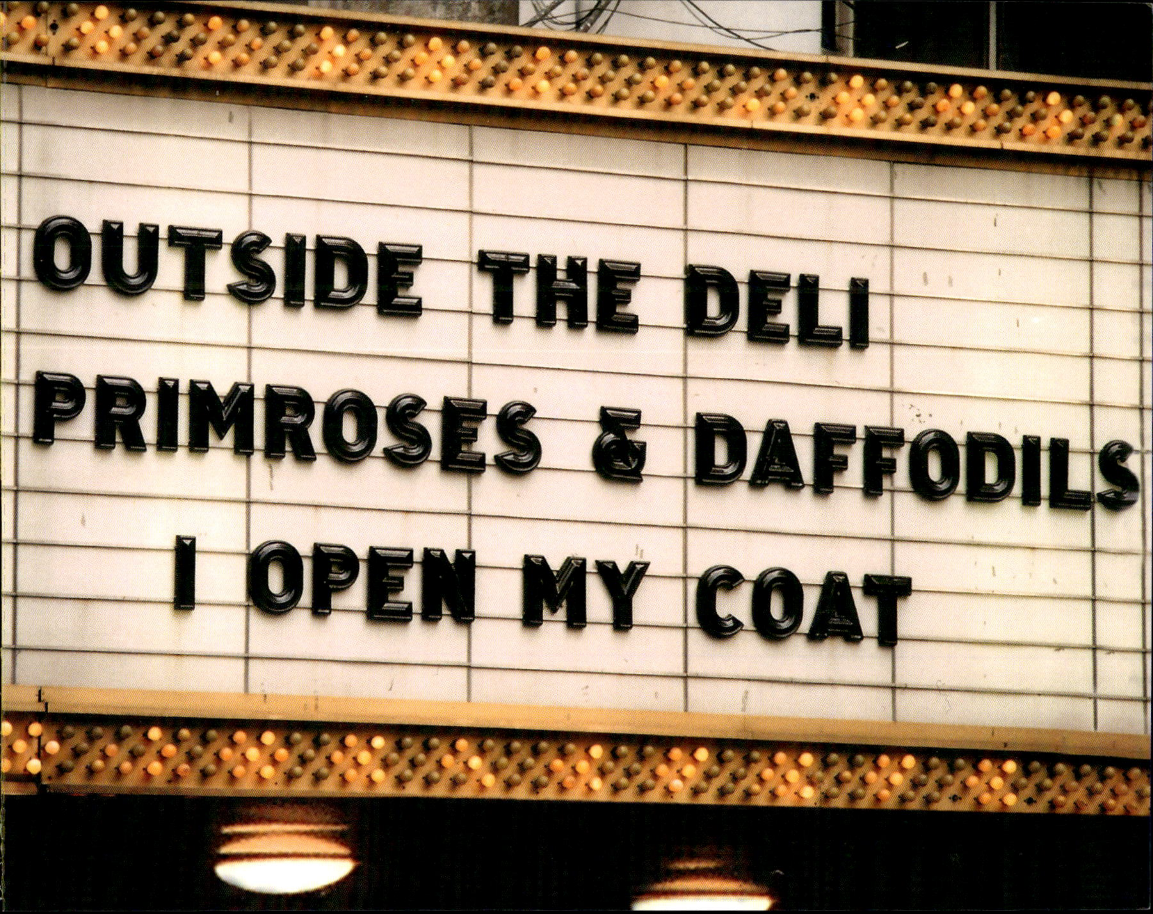
OUTSIDE THE DELI
PRIMROSES & DAFFODILS
I OPEN MY COAT

Outside the deli – haiku by Perdita Finn

Haiku on 42nd Street, Clerisy Press

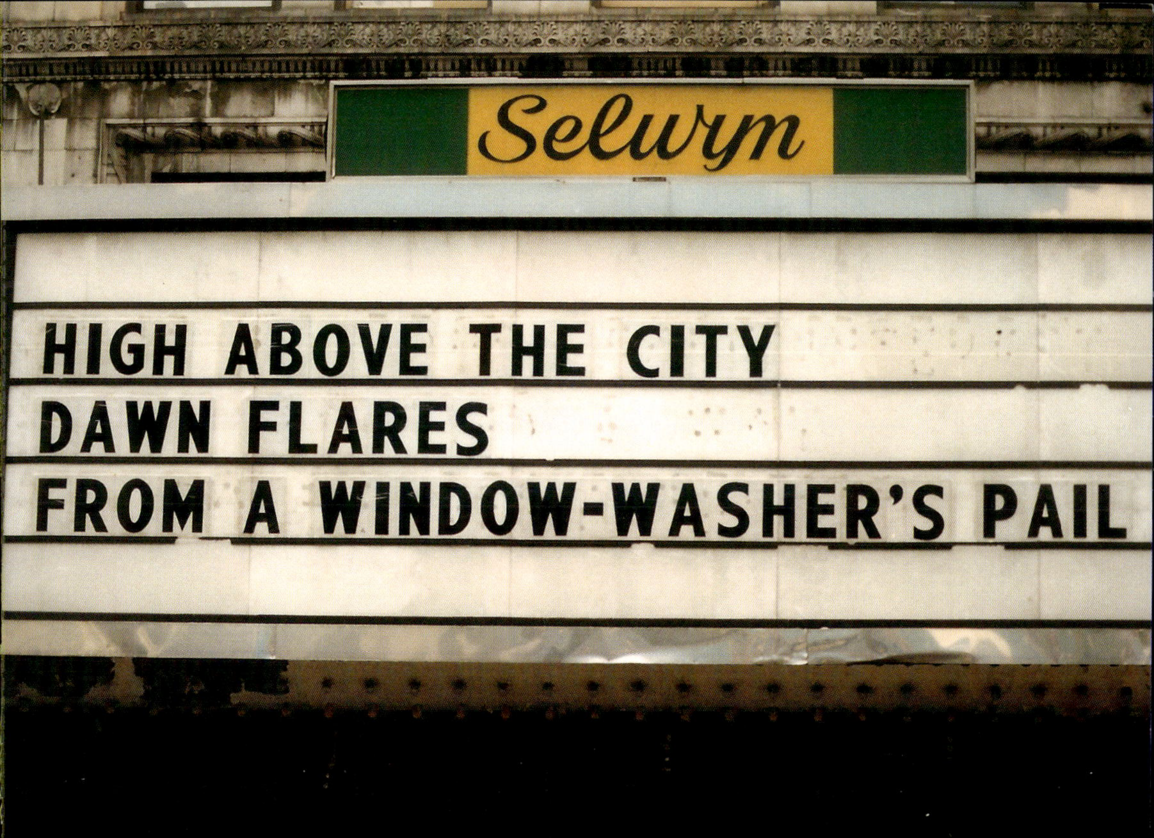
Selwyn
HIGH ABOVE THE CITY
DAWN FLARES
FROM A WINDOW-WASHER'S PAIL

High above the city – haiku by Cor van den Heuvel

Haiku on 42nd Street, Clerisy Press

ALMOST FULL MOON
A LUXURIOUS VOICE
ON THE ANSWERING MACHINE

Almost full moon – haiku by Alexis Rotella

Haiku on 42nd Street, Clerisy Press

BACK FROM THE MOUNTAINS
A YELLOW HANDRAIL
GUIDES ME
DOWN THE SUBWAY STAIRS

Back from the mountain – haiku by Clark Strand

Haiku on 42nd Street, Clerisy Press

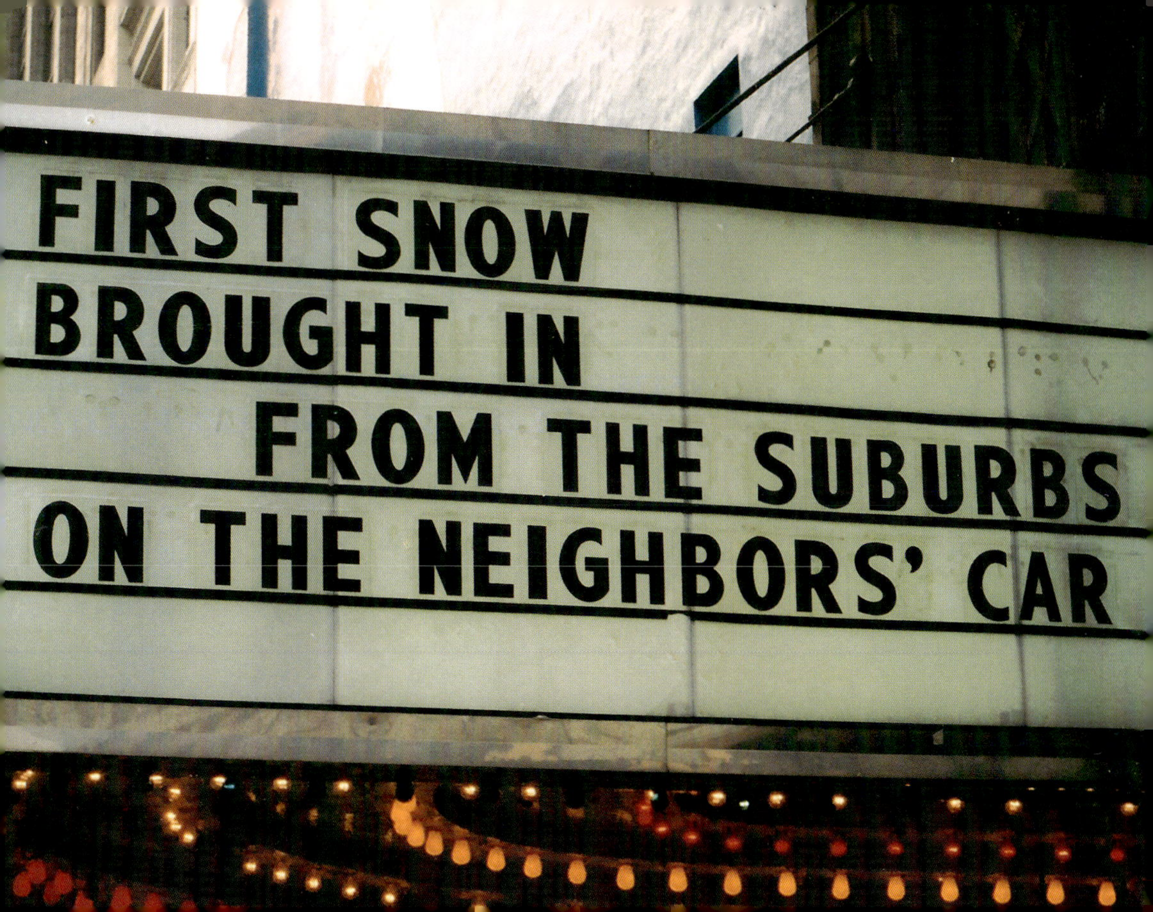
FIRST SNOW
BROUGHT IN
FROM THE SUBURBS
ON THE NEIGHBORS' CAR

First snow – haiku by Doris Heitmeyer

Haiku on 42nd Street, Clerisy Press

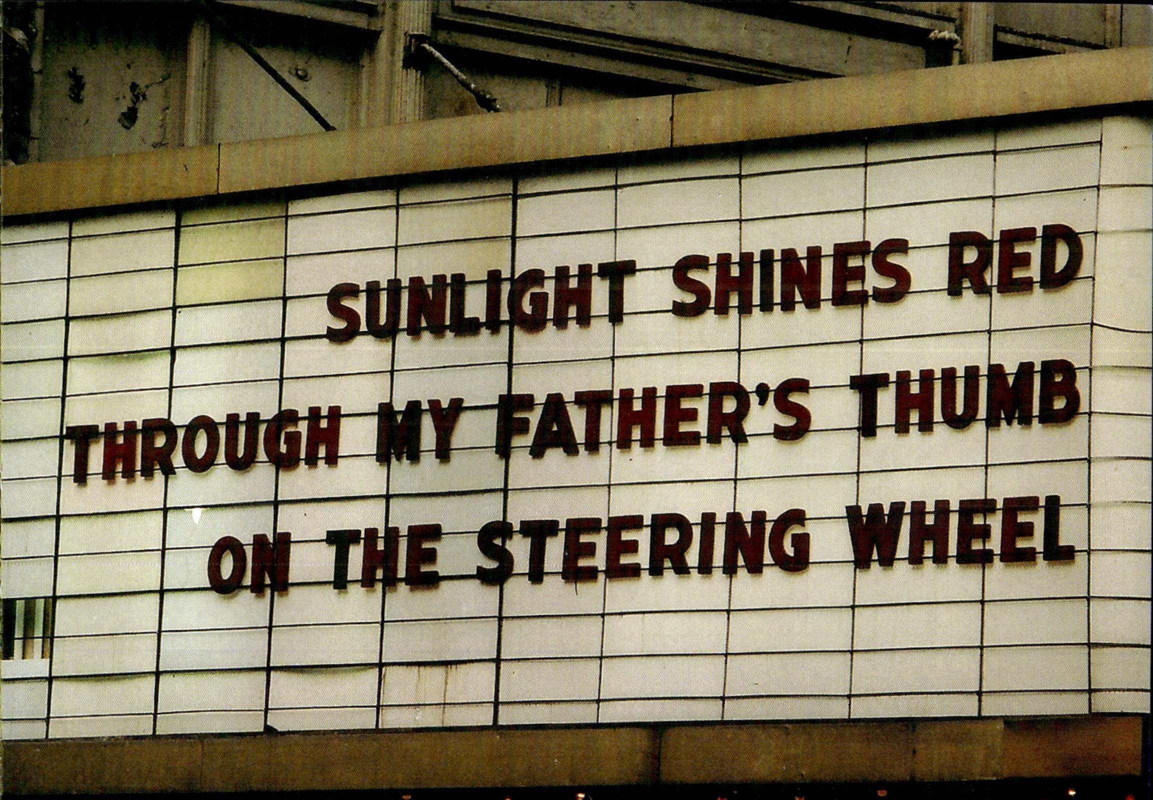
SUNLIGHT SHINES RED
THROUGH MY FATHER'S THUMB
ON THE STEERING WHEEL

Sunlight shines red – haiku by Alyson Pou

Haiku on 42nd Street, Clerisy Press

INTO THE BLINDING SUN
THE FUNERAL PROCESSION'S
GLARING HEADLIGHTS

Into the blinding sun – haiku by Nicholas A. Virgilio

Haiku on 42nd Street, Clerisy Press

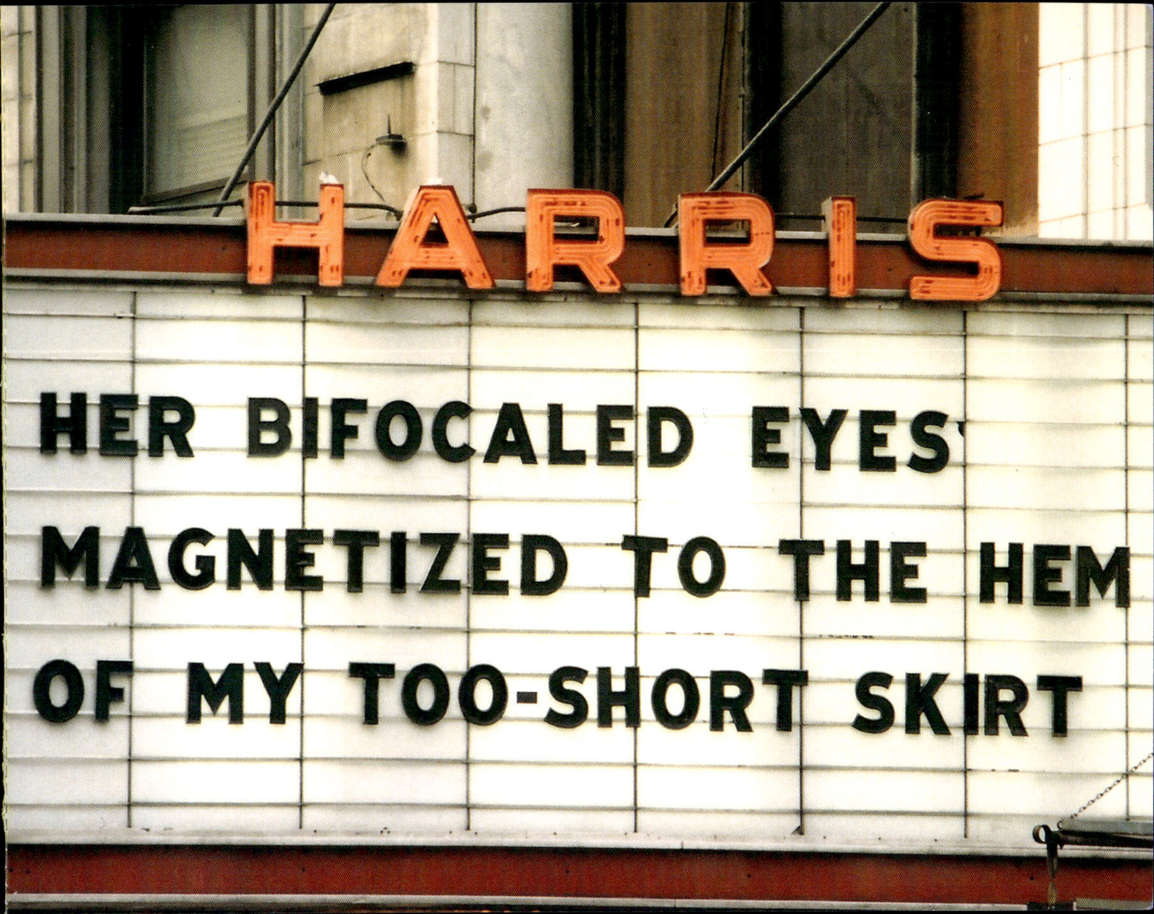
HARRIS
HER BIFOCALED EYES'
MAGNETIZED TO THE HEM
OF MY TOO-SHORT SKIRT

Haiku on 42nd Street, Clerisy Press

CRESCENT MOON
STREET CLOWN BOWS
TO HER LAUGHTER

Crescent Moon – haiku by Anthony J. Pupelllo

Haiku on 42nd Street, Clerisy Press

CONTRIBUTORS

Androgynous—Karen Sohne

Doll hospital—Patricia Neubauer

On the twelfth floor—Martin Burke

Orion—Carl Patrick

City street—Minna Lerman

Car piled with luggage—Yvonne Hardenbrook

Slowly recognizing—Penny Harter

Done—Alan Pizzarelli

In the laundermat—Sydell Rosenberg

Hot day—L.A. Davidson

Between the moon—Adele Kenny

With his clippers—Even Mahl

My reflection—Mykel Board

With a flourish—Dee Evetts

The driver—Anita Virgil

In Greenwich Village—Bernard Lionel Einbond

Going over a bump—William J. Higginson

Outside the deli—Perdita Finn

High above the city—Cor van den Heuvel

Almost full moon—Alexis Rotella

Back from the mountain—Clark Strand

First snow—Doris Heitmeyer

Sunlight shines red—Alyson Pou

Into the blinding sun—Nicholas A. Virgilio

Her bifocaled eyes—Ellen Cowhey

Crescent moon—Anthony J. Pupelllo

Poetry / Gift / New York

Haiku on 42nd St.

Times Square. Crossroads of the world. North America's hotspot for neon lights, Broadway shows and New Year's Eve celebrations. But not so long ago, it wasn't the shiny tourist mecca of today, but instead carried a slightly shabby dignity along with its glorious history of premieres, WWII homecomings and parades.

Almost as advance guard for the transformation, Haiku on 42nd St. magically appeared one night on the abandoned movie marquees. This whimsical collection of wordplay put a smile on the face of everyone who passed by. You hold in your hands the heart of this enterprise with its simple, yet profound, intentions: to find a way to share the serendipity and significance of the project while preserving NYC's moment in time as a public gallery, a crazy state of grace and poetry. Enjoy. Share. Create.

ISBN 978-1-57860-315-2

9 781578 603152 50995>

CLERISY PRESS